Journal Start Date

This Journal Belongs To:

_____

List of parks in this journal:

Journal End Date

AMUSEMENT PARK JOURNAL

An illustrated, lined, diary, notebook with prompts, tips, and tricks to encourage parents, kids, and ride enthusiasts to capture favorite memories and details of their theme park and amusement park visits

By Mike Kunze

Park Hacks Amusement Park Journal
©2020 Mike Kunze
ISBN: 978-0-9986950-6-8
red edition

Published by 2D Fruit Publishing
No part of this publication may be reproduced or transmitted with out the written permission of the publisher.

*This book is dedicated to anyone who misses an extinct attraction.
Horizons at Walt Disney World's EPCOT Center took us to the future.
At the end of last season we lost Vortex at Kings Island. Here's hoping
someday we can ride a Vortex 2 and see "New Horizons!"*

*Parks and children grow and change continuously,
capture each memory while you can.*

How To Use This Journal

This journal is designed to be versatile.

Parents, theme park fans, and serious ride enthusiasts can use these journals to capture what they rode as they visit parks around the world. Children can use them too! Families can record meals, souvenirs, shows, rides, and other activities. Don't forget to write about special moments, like interactions with characters and performers.

The doodles on the pages are there to remind you of things that happened that visit. There are also blank boxes and banners throughout.

You can use these for dates, the name of the park, or when you reach a milestone ride or visit number. It is up to you what and how much you record. Journals are personal.

If you're at your home park, you may want to write down friends you went with or saw, meals you ate, drink flavors you tried, funny moments or memorable things that happened in a show, etc. If you are a ride fan, you might record dates of park visits and the stats of what you rode.

These journals can be carried in the park, or kept in the car or at home to complete afterward. Be sure to capture things that change. Prices of a soft drink typically climb every year or so. Kids also grow, so this can be a great way to record when a child reaches a new height threshold and gets to try a new ride for their first time.

As said in the dedication, amusement parks always change. Parts wear out. Tastes and technologies change. Get the most out of each unique visit by documenting them. Turn memories into keepsakes by collecting them here!

You can record everything...
July 19, 2018 Cedar Point
Stayed in Cedar Point's Express Hotel
Ate breakfast at McDonald's
Entered park at 10 AM
Rode Top Thrill Dragster, Corkscrew,
Rougarou,
Ate Mac n Cheese for lunch
Rode Sky Ride, Valraven
Wind seeker, Gate keeper ...

Or you can record visits and highlights only...
King's Island 7/9 Chicken Salad
Walked a lap of park, Rode Mystic
Timbers and Boo Blaster

King's Island 7/10 Saw show,
walked a lap and enjoyed a drink
by the fountain. Saw old friends...

Or you can track rides like the
Ride Log in the back of the book

Beast	Diamondback	Banshee	Stunt

Capture memories any way you like!

Planning A Trip

Preliminary Research
Check parks' websites for official operating dates and hours. Special events often block normal days at the beginning and end of the season. Follow the blog or other social media channels for other important deals like a Bring-A-Friend day.

Learn the Basic Layout
You don't have to memorize every ride on the map. Getting familiar with the layout of the park can help save valuable time and steps. Is the park long or deep, like Cedar Point, or wide like Kings Island?

Weather
The weather is usually the most important influence for crowds. Rain, thick cloud cover, or steady drizzle can benefit a ride enthusiast with a high number of rides because cold, wet weather keeps the crowds light.

Extra Gear
There are a few other items that would be good to have in the car. Hats, jackets, ponchos and umbrellas can help keep the fun going when the weather changes during the day.

Use Maps
If you're planning to stay in a hotel, open up a maps app and consider all commercial areas within a 30-minute drive. More variety, quality and better prices may be a few minutes away. Also, consider any other nearby attractions you may want to visit while you're in town.

Spare Clothes
It is wise to have each person in your group bring an extra change of clothes… especially socks and underwear! Leave them in the car. If you get wet from rides or weather, a wardrobe change can help you have a comfort evening. You can also buy replacements. Ask a park associate which store sells basic replacement clothing items. There is almost always a handy store that offers these essentials and over-the-counter pain and nausea medicine.

Storing Your Stuff

Is it about safety, or is because parks wand to rent more lockers? Parks have been getting strict on loose articles. In the past, riders could ride roller coasters with sunglasses clutched in one hand and a souvenir drink cup between their feet. Today, most rides don't allow backpacks, hip packs, or purses on rides. How does one carry items they need at the park?

Cargo Shorts
They are the suburban equivalent of Bat Man's utility belt. They feature snaps, zippers and even Velcro to help keep items secure, while offering tons of storage. You can carry your copy of this Park Hacks journal, three phones, a pen, car keys, and a wallet... with room to spare in a sturdy pair of these low-fashion short pants.

Strollers and Wagons
You can usually tuck gear into a pocket or other nooks and crannies. Funny observation, you don't actually need to have a kid! Strollers and wagons serve as a base of operation for many families. Many have cup holders. They can be draped with damp beach towels. They can shelter napping kids, carry diapers and store snacks for the little ones. Some communities have more risk of theft. In others, theft is rare. You could leave a stroller for hours in one spot. They are free mobile lockers!

Leave it in the Car
Travel light and plan strategic breaks to visit your car.

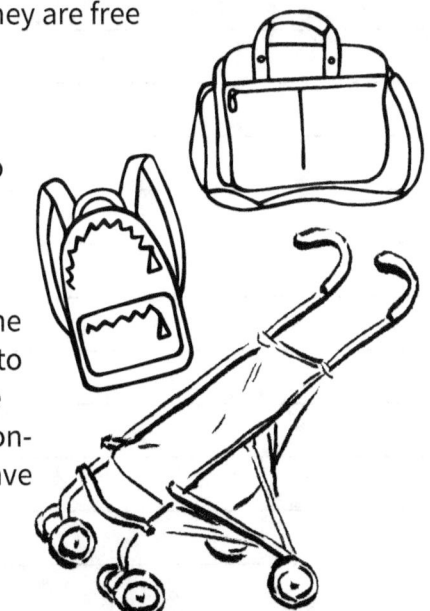

Lockers
Time is precious. It is worth weighing the option of taking a few minutes to walk to the car and back against the cost of the in-park lockers. Lockers that are electronic and managed by a kiosk often can have all-day and hourly pricing options.

Remember, any of these options can hold your Park Hacks journal!

Make a Plan and Stick to It... Mostly

Advanced planning can help you get more out of every visit. Even if it is your home park, think ahead about what you want to do. Share what you care about most. Plans can be simple like getting a burger and fries, followed by walking a full lap of the park. Setting priorities is especially helpful when you go to less familiar parks.

Break the day and park up
Try to focus on one or two specific park area at a time. Time and energy are wasted by crossing the park unnecessarily. Good transitions and planned downtime make the day more satisfying. *They also give you a moment to write in your journal!*

Is one ride, like a brand new roller coaster, a top priority? It can be worth going straight for it when the park gates open. Check to see if you are actually arriving first. Special groups, like season pass holders and resort guests might get earlier admission. Regular visitors can arrive to find long lines already in place. You could instead spend the early part of the day picking off an entire area of the park while it is quiet. But you get to choose!

Plan eating and resting
Shows are fun and they also can provide rest and a place to cool-off. Feeling ill by getting overheated, or doing too many thrill rides back-to-back, can ruin the second half of your day.

If the operating hours are long, get a hand stamp and leave the park for naps or to visit another venue. The water park, a hotel pool, even a nearby store can provide a refresh. There is no shame in taking a nap before returning rested and ready for a special evening of fireworks and nighttime rides.

It is still important to be flexible. Your group may show signs they need rest sooner than expected.

Take note of times when you adapted and were later glad you did.

Letting Children Explore

Parents can use the safe, fun environment of the park to build kids' independence. There are many opportunities to sit nearby and encourage children explore on their own. Pairing up with friends can also be a good way to help shy kids stretch beyond their comfort zone.

Small Steps

You don't need to push too far, too fast. If walking onto a ride by themselves is too much, you can start them off by having them run for ketchup or a few extra napkins when you are preparing to eat. If that goes well, sending them for a drink refill is a good next step.

Phones

More kids are carrying phones. Help kids understand how to keep their phone safe and how to monitor the battery. Some lockers have recharging plugs. You can also teach them to turn the phone off or to leave it on standby to conserve power. Today, kids are not used to experiencing boredom. When they get in a slow queue, out come the phones. Beyond conserving batteries, there are mental benefits of being able to handle a few moments of boredom.

Meeting Places

As they get older and more independent, start testing a longer "leash" by letting them go with friends for more than one ride. Set specific meeting times and places. You can also share what you will be doing, so they don't panic if they beat you to the rendezvous.

Document their developing independence in your journal!

Seasonal Trends

Parks that operate year-round have a constant blend of new and more experienced associates or cast members, which makes the experience more consistent.

Parks that close in the Fall or early Winter, and reopen in the Spring have a more noticeable shift in associate experience. There are many experienced employees around, but during those first cool days of an operating season, it is a good idea to expect a lot of park associates to be a little *green*.

Slow and Careful
The parks have strict rules about rider safety, which is a good thing! New associates have a lot of new training to think about. It takes time for ride operators to develop a rhythm for herding small children through the loading and securing of restraints. Try to stay patient and positive. They get faster and more confident after a day or two of practice.

Fastidious Rule Followers
The other problem that happens when new associates start, is that many turn into little versions of Barney Fife, the legalistic deputy from Andy Griffith. They often lean toward being too cautious and too strict. Kids that measured tall enough to ride weeks ago, may find themselves denied because a different pair of shoes, or a haircut, took them down a fraction of an inch.

It isn't worth fighting a battle. The ride operators are trained to be careful and to take safety seriously. Thank the operator and back away. Try again later. It is also well established that we are taller earlier in the day because our spines compress a little during the day. So if the kid is on the cusp, make sure they remember to wear their thick-soled shoes and a good pair of socks.

Write some of your early season observations in your journal. Then look back later in the season and add updates!

Park Rituals

Does your family have park traditions? Some families arrive in the dark, hours before the park opens on its first day of the season.

Check How They Measure Up
Kids grow! A couple months away is often enough time to see a big leap in growth. A first visit for the season is a great time to note how much they've grown. Record heights and the date. Check again and record their growth at the end of the season as well.

If they cross a height threshold, it may enable new ride options. Make a ceremony out of their first time on a ride. Record the date and time of their first time on each new ride.

What Else Has Changed?
Park associates have been busy making repairs and updates before opening for the new season. It is like a treasure hunt discovering big changes like new rides or restaurants, to subtle updates like signs and restroom fixtures. Noticing what is new can build appreciation for what the staff does behind the scenes.

What Did You Miss The Most?
When you've been away, what is a must do when you return? Is there a favorite ride you want to see first? Is there a special ride that you try to do every visit?

Season Highlights
Are there special events that you never miss? National holidays and the weather can have an unpredictable influence on the park crowds. Sometimes they are light, other times extremely crowded. Are there holidays, like Memorial Day, Independence Day or Labor Day that your family visits a park?

At The End of the Season
What will you miss? Is there a ride that you tearfully visit one last time at the end of the season? If you've made friends with any park associates, stop by and thank them for a great season. Even better, document your praise for them at guest relations!

Level-Up a Ride

Bored at an amusement park? It is hard to imagine if you don't have the luxury of many visits per season. It can happen. Even a thrill ride can become routine after your tenth or twentieth ride.

Roller coasters offer a lot of different sensations by changing the many variables. The same ride on the same day can provide a wildly different experience depending on:
- Which train
- The side of the car
- The temperature
- Early in the day or later
- If you're in the front, middle or back, seats, etc.

Here are several more ways to upgrade the thrill:
- Hands up
- Close your eyes
- Look the "wrong" direction
- Let go, plus lift feet off the floor
- If a ride has two track options, do one track a few times, then switch sides… with your eyes closed!

Name a Challenge

You can choose a challenge or name a quest for a visit. This is best when crowds are light, but it is a fun way to motivate a group into action.

- **Height** - Complete all attractions that are taller than 100 feet
- **Speed** - All the rides that go faster than 50 mph
- **Inversions** - Ride all the rides that go upside-down
- **Wet** - Do all the rides that splash riders with water
- **History** - Go on all rides original to or older than the park
- **Every Seat** - Ride in every seat, on every train of your favorite
- **Big Hour** - How many times you can ride one ride in 60 minutes?
- **First Row** - Do all roller coasters in the front seat

Make sure you document challenges in your journal!

Ride Log

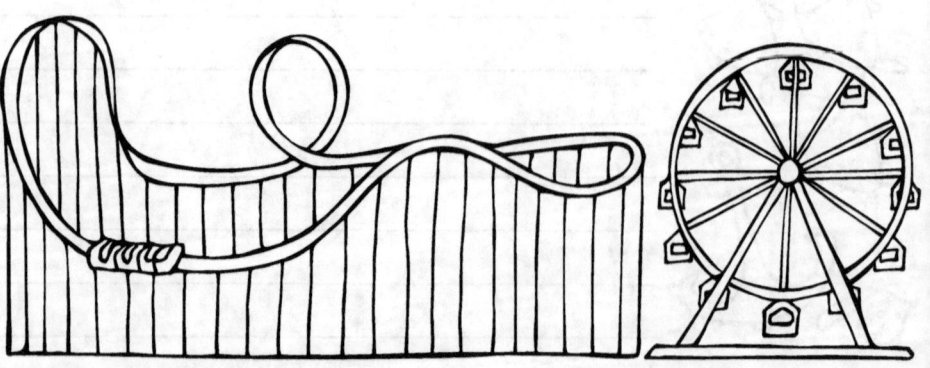

Ride Log

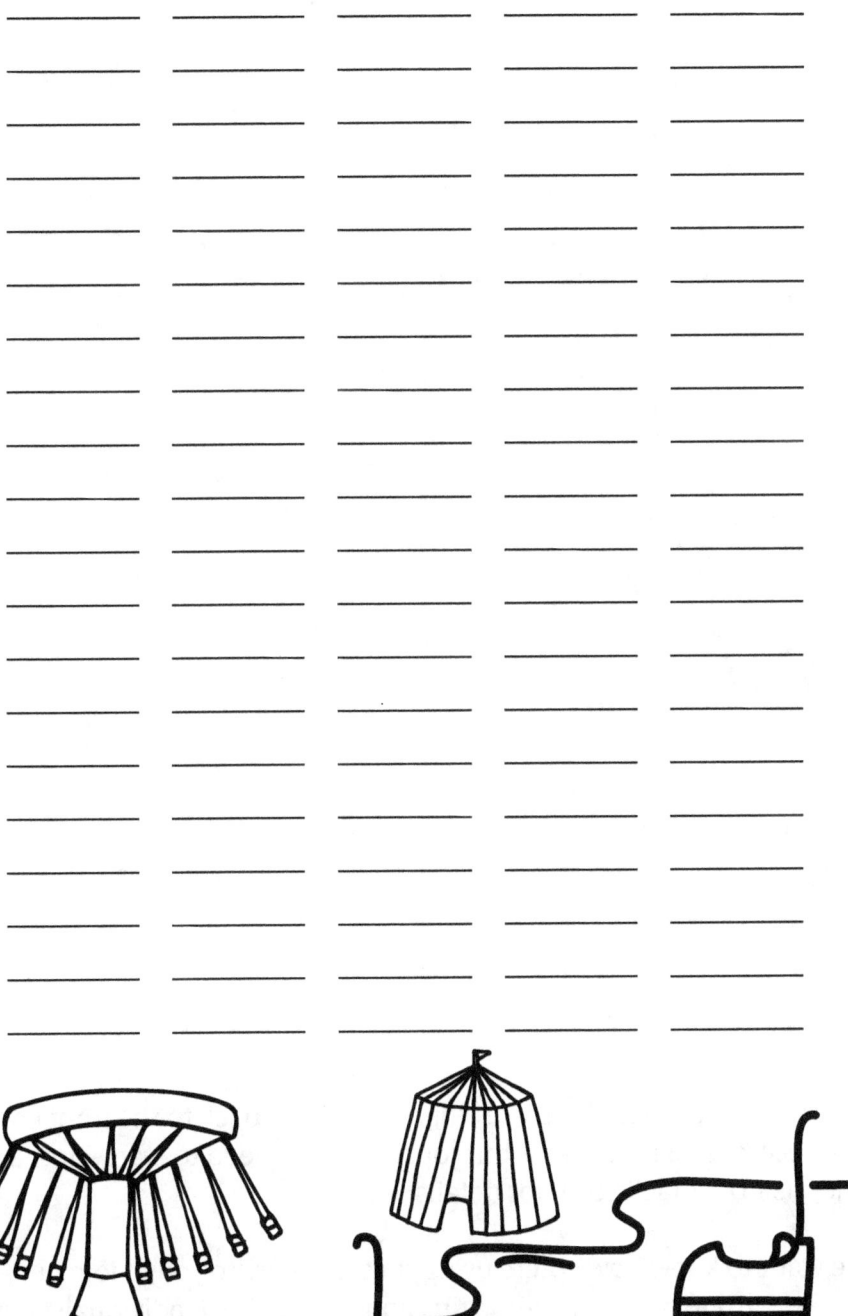

Ride Log

Hey, you've reached the end of this journal! Go back to the front cover and record the end date for this journal. If you need to start another one, visit parkhacks.com for details.

We want to know how you're using these. We invite you to join our Park Hackers group where we share tips and discuss how individuals and families can best enjoy amusement parks and theme parks.

www.ingramcontent.com/pod-product-compliance
Lightning Source LLC
Chambersburg PA
CBHW070441010526
44118CB00014B/2149